BOOK of PRAYERS

The Power of
PRAYING®
for Your
Adult
Children

STORMIE
OMARTIAN

D0710914

HARVEST HOUSE PUBLISHERS
EUGENE, OREGON

THE POWER OF PRAYING® FOR YOUR ADULT CHILDREN BOOK OF PRAYERS
Copyright © 2009, 2014 by Stormie Omartian
Published by Harvest House Publishers
Eugene, Oregon 97402
www.harvesthousepublishers.com

ISBN 978-0-7369-5794-6 (pbk.)
ISBN 978-0-7369-5795-3 (eBook)

Printed in the United States of America

17 18 19 20 21 22 / BP-JH / 10 9 8 7

Introduction

As long as we live, we parents will always have our children on our minds and hearts. Even after they become adults, we will forever be concerned for their safety, well-being, relationship with God, and success in all they do—from their work to their health, to their friends, to their marriage relationship, to the raising of their children. Because we don't know exactly what is going on in their lives, we need a way to pray that will cover them and bring us peace in the process. I have written a book about that called *The Power of Praying for Your Adult Children*, which I passionately invite you to read as well. This little book you are holding contains some of the prayers from that book. It is small enough to carry with you so you can pray whenever your adult children come to mind.

I believe these prayers will help any parent to have a positive impact on the lives of their adult children. I pray that each prayer will help you to find greater freedom from worry and concern because you are tapping into the power of God, which is greater than anything you or they may be facing. When we take our concerns to the Lord—trusting that God hears our prayers and answers them on behalf of our adult children—our prayers will have the power to effect change in their lives. Who among us doesn't want that?

Stormie Omartian

This is the confidence that we have in Him, that if we ask anything according to His will, He hears us. And if we know that He hears us, whatever we ask, we know that we have the petitions that we have asked of Him.

1 JOHN 5:14-15

What Every Parent of an Adult Child Needs to Know

Lord, I know You are the only perfect parent. Thank You for loving my adult children as much as I do. Thank You for hearing my prayers for them. Give me faith to believe and patience to wait for the answers. Help me to not blame myself for anything that goes wrong in their lives. Where I have made mistakes, I confess those to You and ask that You would redeem them all and release me from all guilt. Help me to forgive my adult children for anything they have done to hurt or disappoint me. Today I say, "For this adult child I prayed, and You, Lord, have heard my prayers and granted my petition" (1 Samuel 1:27). I give You all praise and glory.

In Jesus' name I pray.

Continue earnestly in prayer,
being vigilant in it with thanksgiving.

COLOSSIANS 4:2

Prayer Notes

What Every Parent of an Adult Child Needs to Know

Lord, I pray You would teach me how to intercede for my adult children. Thank You that You love me and my children, and that You will hear my prayers for them. Set me free from all worry and concern I have about them so I can have peace. Thank You that Your love and power poured out in me means that my prayers for them will have power. Help me to forgive my adult children's other parent for anything I feel he or she did wrong in raising them. Help me to forgive anyone who has hurt my adult children in any way. Help me to forgive myself for any time I feel that I have not been the perfect parent.

In Jesus' name I pray.

To Him who is able to do exceedingly abundantly above all that we ask or think, according to the power that works in us, to Him be glory in the church by Christ Jesus to all generations, forever and ever.

EPHESIANS 3:20-21

Prayer Notes

_____

_____

_____

_____

_____

_____

_____

_____

_____

_____

_____

See God Pour Out His Spirit upon Them

Lord, You have said that in the last days You will pour out Your Spirit upon all flesh. I cry out to You from the depths of my heart and ask that You would pour out Your Holy Spirit upon my adult children. Pour out Your Spirit upon me and my other family members as well. Pour out Your Spirit on all of my adult children's in-laws, both present and future. Pour out Your Spirit upon whatever difficult circumstances each of my adult children is facing. Be Lord over every part of their lives and every aspect of their beings. Speak to my adult children's hearts and help them to hear from You. Enable them to understand Your leading and direction for their lives.

In Jesus' name I pray.

It shall come to pass in the last days, says God, that I will pour out of My Spirit on all flesh; your sons and your daughters shall prophesy, your young men shall see visions, your old men shall dream dreams.

ACTS 2:17

Prayer Notes

Pray That Your Adult Children Will

See God Pour Out His Spirit upon Them

Lord, open my adult child's ears to hear Your truth so he (she) will reject all lies. Help him (her) to move by the power of Your Spirit. Enable him (her) to rise above the onslaught of evil in our culture. Where he (she) has walked away from You in any way, stretch out Your hand and draw him (her) back. Convict his (her) heart and bring him (her) back to where he (she) should be. May the Holy Spirit poured out on him (her) completely neutralize the power of the enemy attempting to pour out evil in his (her) life. I know You can do far more in my adult child's life than I can ever do, and I invite You to do so.

In Jesus' name I pray.

*If you then, being evil, know how to give
good gifts to your children, how much more
will your heavenly Father give the Holy Spirit
to those who ask Him!*

LUKE 11:13

Prayer Notes

_____

_____

_____

_____

_____

_____

_____

_____

_____

_____

_____

See God Pour Out His Spirit upon Them

Lord, I pray my adult children will never grieve Your Holy Spirit (Ephesians 4:30), but will receive Him as a gift from You (Luke 11:13). Fill them with Your Holy Spirit and pour into them Your peace, hope, faith, truth, and power. Let a spirit of praise arise in their hearts and teach them to worship You in spirit and in truth. If there is anything I can do or should do—or should not do—as my adult children's parent, please make that clear to me so that I will do the right thing. Holy Spirit of truth, reveal the truth that needs to be seen by me and my children. Guide me in my response to them always.

In Jesus' name I pray.

You shall receive power when
the Holy Spirit has come upon you.

ACTS 1:8

Prayer Notes

Develop a Heart for God, His Word, and His Ways

Lord, I pray that (<u>name of adult child</u>) will love Your Word and will feed her (his) soul with it every day. Speak to her (his) heart and breathe life into every word so that it comes alive to her (him). Teach her (him) Your ways and Your laws and enable her (him) to do the right thing. I pray a silencing of the enemy's voice so that she (he) will hear the Holy Spirit speaking to her (his) heart. You have said in Your Word that when someone turns his ear away from hearing the law, even his prayer is an abomination (Proverbs 28:9). I pray that she (he) will never turn a deaf ear to Your laws.

In Jesus' name I pray.

In the way of righteousness is life,
and in its pathway there is no death.

PROVERBS 12:28

Prayer Notes

_____

_____

_____

_____

_____

_____

_____

_____

_____

_____

_____

Develop a Heart for God, His Word, and His Ways

Lord, I pray for (<u>name of adult child</u>) and ask that You would give her (him) a heart to know You. I pray that just as it was said of Your good and faithful servant Daniel that "an excellent spirit was in him" (Daniel 6:3), may it also be said of my daughter (son) that an excellent spirit is in her (him). Draw her (him) close to You and enable her (him) to become more like You. You have said in Your Word that You are the door by which anyone can enter and be saved (John 10:9). Keep her (him) from going through any other door except the path to eternity that You have for her (him).

In Jesus' name I pray.

*For the eyes of the LORD run to and fro
throughout the whole earth,
to show Himself strong on behalf of those
whose heart is loyal to Him.*

2 CHRONICLES 16:9

Prayer Notes

_____

_____

_____

_____

_____

_____

_____

_____

_____

_____

_____

_____

Pray That Your Adult Children Will

Develop a Heart for God, His Word, and His Ways

Lord, where my daughter (son) has walked away from You in any way, cause her (him) to return to You with her (his) whole heart (Jeremiah 24:7). Enable her (him) to become a new creation in Christ as You have said in Your Word (2 Corinthians 5:17). Give her (him) a heart of repentance—the kind of heart that is humble and turned toward You. Wherever there is any rebellion in her (him), I pray that You would create in her (him) a clean heart and renew a right spirit within her (him). Take away all pride that allows her (him) to think that she (he) can live without You. Give her (him) a desire to want what You want.

In Jesus' name I pray.

*If you abide in Me, and My words abide in you,
you will ask what you desire, and it shall be done
for you. By this My Father is glorified, that you
bear much fruit; so you will be My disciples.*

JOHN 15:7-8

Prayer Notes

Pray That Your Adult Children Will

Develop a Heart for God, His Word, and His Ways

God, help (<u>name of adult child</u>) to have a passion for Your presence and Your Word. Help her (him) to sense the presence of Your Holy Spirit guiding her (him). I pray that she (he) will exalt You, love You enough to put You first, and serve You. May the outpouring of the Holy Spirit in her (his) life energize her (his) devotion to You. I pray that she (he) will draw life from her (his) relationship with You. Keep her (him) on Your path so that she (he) is always where You want her (him) to be, doing what You want her (him) to do. Enable me to inspire in her (him) a greater love for You because she (he) sees Your love in me.

In Jesus' name I pray.

*Draw near to God
and He will draw near to you.*

JAMES 4:8

Prayer Notes

Grow in Wisdom, Discernment, and Revelation

Lord, You have said that if we lack wisdom, we are to ask for it and You will give it to us (James 1:5). I come to You asking that You would pour out Your Spirit of wisdom upon (name of adult child). Give him (her) wisdom to always speak the right word to others, to seek godly and wise counsel, to be humble and not prideful, and not be drawn toward the wisdom of the world. Help him (her) to have the kind of sound wisdom that brings discretion, so that it will become life to his (her) soul (Proverbs 3:21-22). Give him (her) wisdom that will help him (her) always make good choices and decisions, and to trust the right people.

In Jesus' name I pray.

The fear of the LORD is the beginning
of knowledge, but fools despise
wisdom and instruction.

PROVERBS 1:7

Prayer Notes

_____

_____

_____

_____

_____

_____

_____

_____

_____

_____

Grow in Wisdom, Discernment, and Revelation

Lord, I pray that (<u>name of adult child</u>) will have wisdom that comes through Your Holy Spirit (1 Corinthians 12:8). Help him (her) to be strong, refusing to fall into the ways of the foolish. Help him (her) to have the wisdom to never blaspheme Your name. Bring strong conviction into his (her) heart whenever he (she) is tempted. Instead, I pray that he (she) will "let the high praises of God" be in his (her) mouth and "a two-edged sword" in his (her) hand (Psalm 149:6). Give him (her) wisdom that guides him (her) away from danger and protects him (her) from evil. Give him (her) a deep sense of the truth, and the ability to take information and make accurate judgments about it.

In Jesus' name I pray.

The law of the wise is a fountain of life,
to turn one away from the snares of death.

PROVERBS 13:14

Prayer Notes

Pray That Your Adult Children Will

Grow in Wisdom, Discernment, and Revelation

Lord, I know that Your Word is the two-edged sword You want in my adult child's hand, so I pray that You would put a love in his (her) heart for the Scriptures and a desire to read the Bible every day. Engrave Your words on his (her) mind and heart so that they become life to him (her). Enable him (her) to retain Your words and keep your commands so he (she) can live (Proverbs 4:4). You have said in Your Word that "a wise man will hear and increase learning, and a man of understanding will attain wise counsel" (Proverbs 1:5). I pray that he (she) will become filled with Your wisdom and able to hear the truth and know it.

In Jesus' name I pray.

If any of you lacks wisdom, let him ask of God,
who gives to all liberally and without reproach,
and it will be given to him.

JAMES 1:5

Prayer Notes

Grow in Wisdom, Discernment, and Revelation

Lord, I pray that You would give my adult child the ability to discern between good and evil, just as You gave that ability to Solomon. Help him (her) to discern between holy and unholy, clean and unclean, right and wrong. Give him (her) insight into people and situations, enabling him (her) to see what he (she) would otherwise not be able to see. Help him (her) to see the things that can only be spiritually discerned (1 Corinthians 2:14). I pray that he (she) will "cry out for discernment" and lift up his (her) voice for understanding so that he (she) will "understand the fear of the LORD and find the knowledge of God" (Proverbs 2:3,5).

In Jesus' name I pray.

*If you cry out for discernment, and lift up
your voice for understanding, if you seek her
as silver, and search for her as for hidden treasures;
then you will understand the fear of the LORD,
and find the knowledge of God.*

PROVERBS 2:3-5

Prayer Notes

_____

_____

_____

_____

_____

_____

_____

_____

_____

_____

_____

Grow in Wisdom, Discernment, and Revelation

Lord, I pray that You would give my adult children revelation for their lives. Help them to be guided by that revelation in all they do. Don't let them become paralyzed with indecision because they don't have a word in their heart from You. Give them revelation that fills their minds and hearts with a vision for their lives that opens their eyes to what Your purpose and calling is for them. Give them the kind of revelation that enables them to make a right decision they would not have made without it. Most of all, I pray You would reveal who You are to them in such a way that they know it is a revelation from You.

In Jesus' name I pray.

Where there is no revelation,
the people cast off restraint;
but happy is he who keeps the law.

PROVERBS 29:18

Prayer Notes

Find Freedom, Restoration, and Wholeness

Lord, I know You are greater than anything my adult child may be shackled by, and Your plans for her (his) life are for total freedom. Holy Spirit, help her (him) to understand that where You are, there is liberty. Help her (him) to find the transformation that can only be found in Your presence. Teach my daughter (son) to seek Your presence in the Word, in prayer, and in praise and worship. Help her (him) to know the truth in Your Word that sets her (him) free. Help her (him) to see the truth about any sin in her (his) life. Where the enemy is oppressing her (him), remove the blinders from her (his) eyes so she (he) can recognize the truth about that too.

In Jesus' name I pray.

*The Lord is the Spirit; and where
the Spirit of the Lord is, there is liberty.*

2 CORINTHIANS 3:17

Prayer Notes

Find Freedom, Restoration, and Wholeness

Lord, I pray that my adult children will find all the freedom and liberty You have for them. I pray for an outpouring of Your Holy Spirit of liberty upon them so that great breakthrough can come in any area of their lives where it is needed. Whether they have been imprisoned by their own sins, or the lies and plans of the enemy have held them captive, I pray You would liberate them. If they need to be set free from a wrong mind-set or an ungodly belief, help them to move into freedom in Christ. I don't know all the ways my adult children need to be set free, but You do, Lord. Please shed Your light on whatever must be illuminated so they can see.

In Jesus' name I pray.

If the Son makes you free,
you shall be free indeed.

JOHN 8:36

Prayer Notes

Find Freedom, Restoration, and Wholeness

Jesus, Your Word says that You came "to proclaim liberty to the captives" and "to set at liberty those who are oppressed" (Luke 4:18). I pray that wherever (name of adult child) has been held captive by anything, You would set her (him) free. Where she (he) is being oppressed by the enemy, I pray that You would deliver her (him) from that torment. Break any stronghold that the enemy has erected against her (him). I know that one of the greatest things I can do for my adult child is to get free myself. Show me if I am entertaining anything in my mind, my heart, or my life that is not of You so I can be free of it.

In Jesus' name I pray.

The angel of the LORD encamps all around those who fear Him, and delivers them.

PSALM 34:7

Prayer Notes

Find Freedom, Restoration, and Wholeness

Lord, I pray You would make whole anything in my adult child's life that is broken. Bring restoration of all that has been lost. Restore lost time, lost opportunities, lost health, lost relationships, or whatever else that has been taken from her (him). Bring the transformation needed so that she (he) can receive the wholeness You have for her (him). Once she (he) has been set free, help her (him) to stay free. Keep her (him) from becoming entangled again. I say to You, Lord, "Be exalted, O God, above the heavens, and Your glory above all the earth; that Your beloved may be delivered" (Psalm 108:5-6).

In Jesus' name I pray.

Stand fast therefore in the liberty by which Christ has made us free, and do not be entangled again with a yoke of bondage.

GALATIANS 5:1

Prayer Notes

_____

_____

_____

_____

_____

_____

_____

_____

_____

_____

_____

Pray That Your Adult Children Will

Find Freedom, Restoration, and Wholeness

Lord, deliver me from everything that hinders the flow of Your Spirit in me. I pray that my freedom will be apparent to my adult children and that it will inspire a desire for freedom in them. Help me to have the kind of dynamic, powerful, and hope-filled relationship with You that instills in them a quest for the same. Enable me to always live Your way so that my adult children and I will reap the benefits of Your mercy toward me (Exodus 20:6). May the blessings of my life, lived according to Your laws, flow to them. Show me how to pray so they can be liberated from everything that keeps them from all You have for them.

In Jesus' name I pray.

Because he has set his love upon Me, therefore
I will deliver him; I will set him on high,
because he has known My name.

Psalm 91:14

Prayer Notes

_____

_____

_____

_____

_____

_____

_____

_____

_____

_____

_____

_____

Pray That Your Adult Children Will

Understand God's Purpose
for Their Lives

Lord, I pray for (<u>name of adult child</u>) to have
a sense of purpose for his (her) life and the ability
to understand that purpose with clarity. Give him
(her) the Spirit of wisdom and revelation so that
the eyes of his (her) understanding will be enlightened. Help him (her) to know what is the hope
of Your calling and what is the exceeding greatness of Your power on his (her) behalf (Ephesians
1:17-19). I pray that Your plans to fulfill the destiny and purpose You have for him (her) will suc-
ceed, and not the plans of the enemy. Enable him
(her) to separate himself (herself) from all the dis-
tractions of this world and turn to You in order to
hear Your voice.

In Jesus' name I pray.

May He grant you according to your heart's desire, and fulfill all your purpose.

Psalm 20:4

Prayer Notes

Pray That Your Adult Children Will

Understand God's Purpose for Their Lives

Lord, show me how to pray specifically for my adult child's purpose, direction, and calling. Give me insight and revelation. Help me to encourage him (her) and give helpful input without being judgmental or overbearing. Where the answer seems to be a long time in coming, help us not to lose heart. Keep us strong in prayer until Your purpose has been fulfilled in his (her) life. Help him (her) to hear Your voice so he (she) has a word in his (her) heart from You. Let it become a springboard propelling him (her) in the right direction. Give him (her) a strong sense of direction and purpose that transcends all fear, hesitation, laziness, defeat, and failure.

In Jesus' name I pray.

We know that all things work together
for good to those who love God, to those
who are the called according to His purpose.

ROMANS 8:28

Prayer Notes

_____

_____

_____

_____

_____

_____

_____

_____

_____

_____

_____

Understand God's Purpose for Their Lives

Lord, when my adult children do have a sense of purpose, I pray that they will not lose it. Give them the wisdom and motivation to take the right steps every day. Enable them to understand what is most important in life, so they can make decisions and choices easily. I pray they will never fail to consider their destiny in every choice they make and in everything they do. Help them to not have their minds made up without consulting You. Keep them from insisting on what they want instead of wanting what You want. Instill in my adult children a desire to always be in the center of Your will.

In Jesus' name I pray.

*[I make]mention of you in my prayers: that
the God of our Lord Jesus Christ, the Father of glory,
may give to you the spirit of wisdom and
revelation in the knowledge of Him, the eyes of
your understanding being enlightened; that you
may know what is the hope of His calling.*

EPHESIANS 1:16-18

Prayer Notes

_____

_____

_____

_____

_____

_____

_____

_____

_____

_____

_____

Pray That Your Adult Children Will

Work Successfully and Have Financial Stability

Lord, I pray Your blessings upon (<u>name of adult child</u>). Bless the work of her (his) hands in every way. Give her (him) a strong sense of purpose so that she (he) is led to the right occupation and is always in the job or position that is Your will for her (his) life. Speak to her (him) about what she (he) was created to do, so that she (he) never wanders from job to job without a purpose. Help her (him) find great purpose in every job she (he) does. Pour out Your Holy Spirit upon her (him) and help her (him) to be "not lagging in diligence, fervent in spirit, serving the Lord" (Romans 12:11).

In Jesus' name I pray.

*Whatever you do, do it heartily,
as to the Lord and not to men.*

COLOSSIANS 3:23

Prayer Notes

_____

_____

_____

_____

_____

_____

_____

_____

_____

_____

_____

_____

Work Successfully and Have Financial Stability

Lord, I pray that my adult child will always do her (his) work for Your glory (Colossians 3:23). Convict her (his) heart if there is ever any temptation to do anything unethical, whether deliberately or unknowingly. Lead her (him) away from all questionable or illegal actions. Help her (him) to always know that whatever gain appears to be hers (his) by unlawful or unethical actions will never be kept, and it will ruin her (his) reputation in the end. I pray that she (he) will be convinced that a good reputation is far more valuable than riches (Jeremiah 17:11). Give my adult children wisdom regarding all money matters. Help them to see danger before anything serious happens. Give them understanding about spending, saving, and investing wisely.

In Jesus' name I pray.

Do you see a man who excels in his work?
He will stand before kings; he will not
stand before unknown men.

PROVERBS 22:29

Prayer Notes

_____
_____
_____
_____
_____
_____
_____
_____
_____
_____
_____

Work Successfully and Have Financial Stability

Lord, protect my adult children so that their finances are not lost, stolen, or wasted. I pray that the enemy will never be allowed to steal, kill, or destroy anything in their lives. I pray that they "do good, that they be rich in good works, ready to give, willing to share, storing up for themselves a good foundation for the time to come, that they may lay hold on eternal life" (1 Timothy 6:18-19). Help them to commit their finances to You so that You will be in charge of them. Help them to get free of debt and to be careful with their spending so that their future is secure.

In Jesus' name I pray.

I have been young, and now am old;
yet I have not seen the righteous forsaken,
nor his descendants begging bread.

PSALM 37:25

Prayer Notes

Work Successfully and Have Financial Stability

Lord, enable my adult child to be a good steward of all you have given her (him). Help her (him) to learn to give to You in a way that is pleasing in Your sight. If she (he) is having financial problems right now, I pray for things to turn around. Open the doors of opportunity and help her (him) to find favor in the workplace. Help her (him) to be fairly compensated for the work she (he) does. I pray for Your blessing of provision upon (name of adult child). Give her (him) wisdom with regard to work, career, occupation, and profession. I pray for success in the work You have called her (him) to do.

In Jesus' name I pray.

Every man should eat and drink and enjoy
the good of all his labor—it is the gift of God.

ECCLESIASTES 3:13

Prayer Notes

Pray That Your Adult Children Will

Work Successfully and Have Financial Stability

Lord, You have said to "seek the kingdom of God, and all these things shall be added to you" (Luke 12:31). Help my adult children to surrender to You in body, mind, soul, and spirit so they can move into the abundance and prosperity You have for them. Help them to learn from the correction and instruction of wise teachers and people of maturity, wisdom, and experience so that they will avoid poverty and embarrassment and gain the honor and prosperity You have for them (Proverbs 13:18). I pray that the beauty of the Lord will be upon them and establish the work of their hands (Psalm 90:17). May they "long enjoy the work of their hands" and "not labor in vain" (Isaiah 65:22-23).

In Jesus' name I pray.

When you eat the labor of your hands,
you shall be happy, and it shall be well with you.

PSALM 128:2

Prayer Notes

Have a Sound Mind and a Right Attitude

Lord, I pray that You would help (<u>name of adult child</u>) to be able to take control of his (her) mind and emotions. Enable him (her) to bring every thought into captivity (2 Corinthians 10:5). Help him (her) not to entertain just any thought that comes into his (her) head, but to have the discernment to recognize the voice of the enemy speaking lies. Take away all deception so that he (she) will not accept a lie for truth. Help him (her) to clearly recognize the enemy's deception for the purpose of destroying him (her). Give him (her) the ability to resist filling his (her) mind with anything that is not glorifying to You. Help him (her) to instead fill his (her) mind with thoughts that please You.

In Jesus' name I pray.

Let this mind be in you which was
also in Christ Jesus.

PHILIPPIANS 2:5

Prayer Notes

_____
_____
_____
_____
_____
_____
_____
_____
_____
_____
_____
_____

Pray That Your Adult Children Will

Have a Sound Mind and a Right Attitude

Lord, help (<u>name of adult child</u>) to think about things that are true, noble, just, pure, lovely, good, virtuous, and praiseworthy (Philippians 4:8). I pray for him (her) to be able to resist any attempt of the enemy to torment his (her) mind with negative thoughts and emotions. Help him (her) to be repulsed by ungodly books, magazines, music, films, and Internet and television images so that he (she) always turns away from those things. Help him (her) to choose the love, power, and sound mind You have given him (her). Dissolve any dark clouds of negative emotions that hover over him (her). Set him (her) free from all confusion and bring clarity of mind.

In Jesus' name I pray.

You should no longer walk as the rest of the Gentiles walk, in the futility of their mind, having their understanding darkened, being alienated from the life of God, because of the ignorance that is in them, because of the blindness of their heart...be renewed in the spirit of your mind.

EPHESIANS 4:17-18,23

Prayer Notes

Have a Sound Mind and a Right Attitude

Lord, give my adult child faith to replace all doubt. Bring Your joy where there is sadness or depression. Give him (her) confidence in You to replace insecurity within himself (herself). Give him (her) peace, patience, and forgiveness to replace all anger. Give him (her) Your love to dissolve all fear. Give him (her) Your presence to erase all loneliness. I pray that You would give him (her) wisdom about what he (she) allows into his (her) mind. Give him (her) great discernment so the lines between good and bad are clearly seen. Convict him (her) whenever he (she) crosses the line, and grieve his (her) spirit the way it grieves Yours. I pray for his (her) mind to be captured by You.

In Jesus' name I pray.

Do not be conformed to this world, but be transformed by the renewing of your mind, that you may prove what is that good and acceptable and perfect will of God.

ROMANS 12:2

Prayer Notes

Pray That Your Adult Children Will

Have a Sound Mind and a Right Attitude

Lord, I know that "death and life are in the power of the tongue" (Proverbs 18:21), so I pray that You would help me to always speak words of life to my adult child's mind and heart whenever I talk to him (her). Enable me to build him (her) up and show love in ways he (she) can perceive. Draw my adult child to Your Word so that it will be "a discerner of the thoughts and intents of the heart" every time he (she) reads it (Hebrews 4:12). Reveal to him (her) any wrong thinking or beliefs. Make Your thoughts to be his (her) thoughts. Help him (her) to have the "mind of Christ" at all times and in every situation (1 Corinthians 2:16).

In Jesus' name I pray.

You will keep him in perfect peace, whose mind is stayed on You, because he trusts in You.

ISAIAH 26:3

Prayer Notes

Have a Sound Mind and a Right Attitude

Lord, where my adult child is struggling in his (her) mind or emotions, I pray that You would help him (her) to understand that "weeping may endure for a night, but joy comes in the morning" (Psalm 30:5). May Your peace rule in his (her) heart and cause him (her) to have a grateful attitude toward You (Colossians 3:15). I pray that he (she) will trust in You and be able to say as David did, "Surely I have calmed and quieted my soul" (Psalm 131:2). I claim the "sound mind" You have promised for my adult child. Teach him (her) to lift up praise and worship to You until he (she) hears Your voice clearly speaking to his (her) soul.

In Jesus' name I pray.

Be anxious for nothing, but in everything by prayer and supplication, with thanksgiving, let your requests be made known to God; and the peace of God, which surpasses all understanding, will guard your hearts and minds through Christ Jesus.

PHILIPPIANS 4:6-7

Prayer Notes

Resist Evil Influences and Destructive Behavior

Lord, I pray that You will give (<u>name of adult child</u>) the discernment she (he) needs to understand the clear choice between good and evil, and right and wrong, between what is life giving and life destroying, and between a path into a secure and good future and a dead-end street. I pray that she (he) will not allow the world to shape her (him), but instead she (he) would be shaped by You. I know that the influence of the enemy can come in so subtly as to be nearly unobserved until it's too late. But I pray that with Holy Spirit–given wisdom and discernment she (he) can be prepared for the enemy and anticipate his plans.

In Jesus' name I pray.

The LORD is my rock and my fortress
and my deliverer; my God,
my strength, in whom I will trust.

PSALM 18:2

Prayer Notes

Pray That Your Adult Children Will

Resist Evil Influences and Destructive Behavior

Lord, I pray that this worldly culture will not have a hold on my daughter (son). Sever any attachment in her (him) for the evil of the world and free her (him) to be attached only to You. Protect her (him) from every attack of the enemy. Help her (him) to trust in You and Your power and not "give place to the devil" (Ephesians 4:27). I pray that she (he) would seek Your guidance for her (his) life. I pray that You would be her (his) "hiding place" where she (he) will be preserved from trouble. Surround her (him) "with songs of deliverance" and instruct her (him) in the way she (he) should go (Psalm 32:7).

In Jesus' name I pray.

Trust in the LORD with all your heart,
and lean not on your own understanding;
in all your ways acknowledge Him,
and He shall direct your paths.

PROVERBS 3:5-6

Prayer Notes

_____

_____

_____

_____

_____

_____

_____

_____

_____

_____

_____

Resist Evil Influences and Destructive Behavior

Lord, I pray that You would give me wisdom to know how to pray for each of my adult children. Give me courage to confront them when I need to. Help me to wait for the right timing and give me the exact words to say. Open their hearts to hear from me. Wherever they have strayed from Your ways, I pray You would extend Your shepherd's crook and bring them back into the fold. Be their strength in time of trouble and deliver them from the wicked one (Psalm 37:39-40). Thank You, Lord, that You deliver us from our enemies (Psalm 18:48). Where my adult children have been taken captive by evil influences or destructive behavior, I pray that You will set them free.

In Jesus' name I pray.

*"Not by might nor by power,
but by My Spirit," says the LORD of hosts.*

ZECHARIAH 4:6

Prayer Notes

Resist Evil Influences and Destructive Behavior

Lord, I realize I don't know everything going on in my adult child's mind, emotions, or life, but You do. Reveal what needs to be revealed. Expose any error of thought so clearly that she (he) is brought to repentance before You. Don't allow her (him) to get away with anything. Wherever she (he) is even toying with something that is an enemy trap for her (his) destruction, I pray You would rescue her (him) out of it. Keep her (him) away from people who intend to do evil or involve her (him) in evil works. Keep her (him) from falling into temptation. Strengthen her (him) to resist all evil influences and avoid all destructive behavior. Keep and protect her (him) from the evil one.

In Jesus' name I pray.

For the weapons of our warfare are not carnal but mighty in God for pulling down strongholds.

2 Corinthians 10:4

Prayer Notes

Resist Evil Influences and Destructive Behavior

Lord, work in my adult child's life to bring her (him) into full alignment with Your will. Open her (his) eyes to see Your truth, so she (he) will be free of any deception. Smash any false idols in her (his) mind that entice her (him) off the path You have for her (him). I know that You will not violate the will of my adult child, but I invite You to penetrate her (his) life by the power of Your Holy Spirit and cause her (his) heart to be touched by Your presence. I pray that she (he) will be free of all evil influences and destructive behavior.

In Jesus' name I pray.

*You who love the LORD, hate evil! He preserves
the souls of His saints; He delivers them out of the
hand of the wicked. Light is sown for the righteous,
and gladness for the upright in heart.*

PSALM 97:10-11

Prayer Notes

Avoid All Sexual Pollution and Temptation

Lord, help my adult child to flee sexual pollution—to turn away from it, not look at it, and not be drawn into it. Give him (her) the conviction to change the channel; shut down the website; throw out the magazine, DVD, or CD; or walk out of the theater (Proverbs 27:12). Give him (her) understanding that any deviation from the path You have for him (her)—even if it is only occurring in the mind—will be a trap to fall into and a snare for his (her) soul. Enable him (her) to stand on the solid ground of purity in Your sight. Help him (her) to hide Your Word in his (her) heart so that he (she) will not sin against You (Psalm 119:9-11).

In Jesus' name I pray.

*For all that is in the world—the lust of the flesh,
the lust of the eyes, and the pride of life—
is not of the Father but is of the world.*

1 John 2:16

Prayer Notes

_____

_____

_____

_____

_____

_____

_____

_____

_____

_____

Avoid All Sexual Pollution and Temptation

Lord, I pray for (<u>name of adult child</u>) to be free of all sexual pollution. Wherever he (she) has seen things that have compromised his (her) sexual purity, I pray You would cleanse his (her) mind of it and take it out of his (her) heart. If he (she) has become involved in anything that violates Your standards for purity, I pray that You would convict his (her) conscience about it and bring him (her) to repentance before You. Enable him (her) to stand on the solid ground of purity in Your sight. Help him (her) to see that even unintended disobedience to Your ways will require a cleansing on his (her) part. I pray You would set him (her) completely free from any ungodly desires.

In Jesus' name I pray.

Who may ascend into the hill of the LORD?
Or who may stand in His holy place? He who has
clean hands and a pure heart, who has not lifted
up his soul to an idol, nor sworn deceitfully.

PSALM 24:3-4

Prayer Notes

Avoid All Sexual Pollution and Temptation

Lord, where my adult child has allowed any ungodly desires, I pray You would set him (her) free. Put a desire in his (her) heart to please You by walking in the Spirit and not the flesh (Romans 8:8). Help him (her) to know that You are his (her) refuge and he (she) can turn to You any-time temptation is presenting itself (Psalm 141:8). Help him (her) to understand the greatness of Your power to set him (her) free. Turn his (her) eyes away from worthless things (Psalm 119:37). Give him (her) the ability to truly ponder every-thing he (she) does and every step taken so that he (she) will not walk in the path of evil, but in the path You have for him (her) (Proverbs 4:26-27).

In Jesus' name I pray.

*Walk in the Spirit, and you
shall not fulfill the lust of the flesh.*

GALATIANS 5:16

Prayer Notes

Pray That Your Adult Children Will

Avoid All Sexual Pollution and Temptation

Lord, You have said that sin happens just by looking at something bad (Matthew 5:28). But You also gave us a way to get rid of the propensity for it (Matthew 5:29). Wherever there has been any moral failure on my adult child's part, give him (her) a heart of repentance so that he (she) can come before You and be cleansed of all the effects and consequences of it. I pray that he (she) will never be seduced down a path that leads to destruction. Enable him (her) to resist all temptation. Give him (her) the "spirit of wisdom and revelation" so that he (she) will understand the purpose for which he (she) was created and not want to violate it (Ephesians 1:17-18).

In Jesus' name I pray.

*You are a chosen generation, a royal priesthood,
a holy nation, His own special people, that you
may proclaim the praises of Him who called you
out of darkness into His marvelous light.*

1 Peter 2:9

Prayer Notes

Avoid All Sexual Pollution and Temptation

Lord, I pray that my adult children will get rid of anything in their lives that causes them to compromise the purity of soul that You want. Don't let the light in their eyes die because of seeing sexual pollution. Help them to look to You instead (Psalm 123:1). Enable them to say as David did, "I will set nothing wicked before my eyes" (Psalm 101:3). I pray for a breaking down of the idols of sexual promiscuity, pornography, perversion, sensuality, and immorality in the media, in our land, in our homes, and in our lives. I pray especially that my adult children will not be tempted, trapped, swayed, or polluted by any of it. I pray that You will protect them.

In Jesus' name I pray.

A prudent man foresees evil and hides himself;
the simple pass on and are punished.

PROVERBS 27:12

Prayer Notes

Experience Good Health and God's Healing

Lord, I pray that (<u>name of adult child</u>) will learn to pray in power for her (his) own healing. Raise up in her (him) great faith in the name of Jesus. Give her (him) the understanding to claim the healing that was achieved at the cross. Any place in her (his) body where there is sickness, disease, infirmity, or injury, I pray You would touch her (him) and bring complete healing. Help her (him) to not give up praying until she (he) sees the total healing You have for her (him). Whether her (his) healing is instantaneous or it manifests in a gradual recuperation, I thank You in advance for the miracle of healing You will do in her (his) body.

In Jesus' name I pray.

Heal me, O LORD, and I shall be healed; save me,
and I shall be saved, for You are my praise.

JEREMIAH 17:14

Prayer Notes

Pray That Your Adult Children Will

Experience Good Health
and God's Healing

Lord, I pray that (<u>name of adult child</u>) will enjoy good health and a long life. Give her (him) the wisdom and knowledge necessary to recognize that her (his) body is the temple of Your Holy Spirit and that it should be cared for and nurtured and not disregarded or mistreated. Help her (him) to value good health as a gift from You to be protected and not squandered on foolish or careless living or taken for granted. Teach her (him) how to make wise choices and to reject anything that undermines good health. Reveal any truth that needs to be seen, and give her (him) understanding. Teach her (him) to be disciplined in the way of eating, exercising, and getting proper rest.

In Jesus' name I pray.

*If you diligently heed the voice of the LORD your
God and do what is right in His sight, give ear to
His commandments and keep all His statutes, I will
put none of the diseases on you which I have brought
on the Egyptians. For I am the LORD who heals you.*

EXODUS 15:26

Prayer Notes

_____

_____

_____

_____

_____

_____

_____

_____

_____

_____

_____

Experience Good Health and God's Healing

Lord, help my adult child to bring her (his) body into submission (1 Corinthians 9:27). Help her (him) to recognize any place where she (he) has given place to careless health care habits that are destroying her (his) life. Help her (him) to value her (his) body enough to take care of it, and teach her (him) the right way to live. When she (he) is hurt or not feeling well, guide all doctors who see and treat her (him). Enable them to make the correct diagnosis and to know exactly what to do. Where healing seems to be a long time in coming, help us to not lose heart or hope, but to instead increase the fervency and frequency of our prayers.

In Jesus' name I pray.

He was wounded for our transgressions,
He was bruised for our iniquities; the chastisement
for our peace was upon Him, and by
His stripes we are healed.

ISAIAH 53:5

Prayer Notes

Experience Good Health and God's Healing

Lord, help my daughter (son) to be a good steward of her (his) body. Help her (him) to know that she (he) should present her (his) body as a living sacrifice, holy and acceptable to You (Romans 12:1). Enable her (him) to understand the idea of glorifying You in the care of her (his) body, because it is Your dwelling place. Whenever she (he) is sick, I pray You would be her (his) Healer. Restore health to her (him) and heal all wounds (Jeremiah 30:17). Give her (him) the knowledge and faith to say, "O LORD my God, I cried out to You, and You healed me" (Psalm 30:2). I know that when You heal us, we are truly healed (Jeremiah 17:14).

In Jesus' name I pray.

Bless the LORD, O my soul, and forget not
all His benefits: who forgives all your iniquities,
who heals all your diseases, who redeems
your life from destruction, who crowns
you with lovingkindness and tender mercies.

PSALM 103:2-4

Prayer Notes

Enjoy a Successful Marriage and Raise Godly Children

Lord, I pray for (<u>name of adult child</u>) and ask that You would give him (her) the perfect wife (husband). Bring a godly believing woman (man) into his (her) life, who will be with him (her) for the rest of their lives in a fulfilling and happy marriage. I pray that she (he) will have purity of heart, plus a nature and character that is gracious, kind, giving, and loving. I pray that they will always be attracted to one another in a way that is lasting. I pray above all that they will have great and lasting love for one another. Dwell in their marriage, Lord, and make it what You want it to be.

In Jesus' name I pray.

Unless the LORD builds the house,
they labor in vain who build it.

PSALM 127:1

Prayer Notes

_____
_____
_____
_____
_____
_____
_____
_____
_____
_____
_____
_____
_____

Pray That Your Adult Children Will

Enjoy a Successful Marriage and Raise Godly Children

Lord, for my adult child who is already married, I pray that You will cause him (her) and his (her) mate to increase in love, joy, peace, patience, kindness, goodness, faithfulness, gentleness, and self-control (Galatians 5:22-23). I pray that their hearts will grow close together and not apart. Make the necessary changes in them that are needed. Help each one of them to learn to pray in power for one another. I pray that they will love one another, honor one another, and submit to one another (1 Peter 5:5). Help them to communicate mutual appreciation and respect. I pray that forgiveness will flow easily between them and that no negative emotions will spoil the atmosphere of their home.

In Jesus' name I pray.

*Above all things have fervent love for one another,
for "love will cover a multitude of sins."*

1 PETER 4:8

Prayer Notes

Enjoy a Successful Marriage and Raise Godly Children

Lord, help my adult child to be the best husband (wife) possible. Teach him (her) the things needed to make a marriage successful. Give him (her) understanding, patience, and the ability to communicate well. I pray that there will be no pride in him (her) that would stir up strife, but rather he (she) would trust in You and be prospered (Proverbs 28:25). Take out of his (her) life anything that would keep him (her) from becoming the husband (wife) You want him (her) to be. I pray that his (her) heart will be kind and soft toward his (her) spouse, and that they will always be each other's top priority. I pray there will be no divorce in their future.

In Jesus' name I pray.

What God has joined together,
let not man separate.

MATTHEW 19:6

Prayer Notes

_____

_____

_____

_____

_____

_____

_____

_____

_____

_____

_____

Enjoy a Successful Marriage and Raise Godly Children

Lord, I pray that my adult children will have healthy, whole, intelligent, gifted, and godly children. Help them through every step of parenthood and enable them to be successful in raising children who are obedient, bright, healthy, happy, and productive. As parents, give them an abundance of love, patience, understanding, and wisdom. Guide them every step of the way, through every stage of each child's development. I pray that they will look to You for guidance so that they will train up their children in Your ways. Teach them how to discipline, correct, guide, and nurture their children properly. Help them to always recognize that their children are a gift from You. I pray that their relationship with each child will be good and lasting.

In Jesus' name I pray.

*They shall not labor in vain, nor bring forth
children for trouble; for they shall be
the descendants of the blessed of the LORD,
and their offspring with them.*

ISAIAH 65:23

Prayer Notes

Enjoy a Successful Marriage and Raise Godly Children

Lord, protect each of my adult children's children from all harm and any plans of evil. Protect them from injury or disease. Help them to know You and learn to live Your way. Do not allow them to live separated from You. Give them a humble and teachable spirit, and help them to always honor and obey their parents and not fall into rebellion. Help me to leave a great inheritance to my children and their children in terms of wisdom, godliness, fruitfulness, and wholeness that will bless them for their entire lives (Proverbs 13:22). Help me to live a godly life that pleases You, so that I will not only know Your mercy, but they will know it as well (Psalm 103:17-18).

In Jesus' name I pray.

The mercy of the LORD is from everlasting to everlasting on those who fear Him, and His righteousness to children's children, to such as keep His covenant, and to those who remember His commandments to do them.

PSALM 103:17-18

Prayer Notes

_____

_____

_____

_____

_____

_____

_____

_____

_____

_____

_____

Maintain Strong and Fulfilling Relationships

Lord, I pray (<u>name of adult child</u>) will have friends who tell her (him) the truth in love (Proverbs 27:6). I pray for friends who are wise (Proverbs 13:20) and will always be a strong support for her (him) (Ecclesiastes 4:9-10). I pray that each relationship in her (his) life will be glorifying to You. I pray also for good relationships with parents, siblings, and other family members. Bless these relationships with deep love, great compassion, mutual understanding, and good communication. Where there are breeches or rough spots in any one of those relationships, I pray that You would bring peace, healing, and reconciliation. I pray that the enemy will not be able to break apart any relationships or friendships.

In Jesus' name I pray.

If we walk in the light as He is in the light, we have fellowship with one another, and the blood of Jesus Christ His Son cleanses us from all sin.

1 JOHN 1:7

Prayer Notes

Pray That Your Adult Children Will

Maintain Strong and Fulfilling Relationships

Lord, I pray for my adult child to have godly friends in her (his) life. I pray that they will give her (him) good advice and guidance (Proverbs 27:9) and be a positive influence on her (him). Enable her (him) to see the truth about people and be drawn toward those who are good. I pray specifically for her (his) relationship with (name of person). I pray that You would help them to always have harmony with one another by the power of Your Holy Spirit. If there is ever any miscommunication, bring clarity and good communication. If there is ever a rightful grievance, bring repentance and apologies. If the relationship breaks down, for whatever reason, bring healing and restoration.

In Jesus' name I pray.

I am a companion of all who fear You,
and of those who keep Your precepts.

PSALM 119:63

Prayer Notes

_____
_____
_____
_____
_____
_____
_____
_____
_____
_____
_____
_____

Pray That Your Adult Children Will

Maintain Strong and Fulfilling Relationships

Lord, I pray that my adult child will always have good relationships with coworkers. Where there is a coworker who is ungodly, I pray that my adult child will be a godly influence on that person. I pray that she (he) will walk with the wise and become wiser, and not be a "companion of fools" and be destroyed (Proverbs 13:20). Help her (him) to also learn the obedience of forgiveness. Enable her (him) to forgive easily and not carry grudges, resentment, bitterness, or a personal list of wrongs. Help her (him) to release unforgiveness quickly to others, so that it never interferes with her (his) relationship with You and delays the forgiveness she (he) needs for her (his) own life (Mark 11:25).

In Jesus' name I pray.

Be kind to one another, tenderhearted,
forgiving one another, even as
God in Christ forgave you.

EPHESIANS 4:32

Prayer Notes

Pray That Your Adult Children Will

Be Protected and Survive Tough Times

Lord, I pray that You would surround my adult children with Your angels to keep watch over them so that they will not stumble (Psalm 91:12). Help them to hear Your voice leading them, and teach them to obey You so that they will always be in Your will and at the right place at the right time. I pray that "the fear of the LORD" will be for them a "fountain of life" that will serve to turn them "away from the snares of death" (Proverbs 14:27). I pray that You will keep Your eyes on them and that they will not take their eyes off of You. Help them to learn to dwell in Your shadow where they are protected (Psalm 91:1).

In Jesus' name I pray.

*The LORD shall preserve your going out
and your coming in from this time forth,
and even forevermore.*

PSALM 121:8

Prayer Notes

Be Protected and Survive Tough Times

Lord, I pray for Your hand of protection to be over my adult children. I pray that they will put their trust in You as their shield and protector (Proverbs 30:5). Protect them physically from all accidents, diseases, infirmity, acts of violence by others, sudden dangers, and the plans of evil. Be their protector whenever they are in a car, plane, bus, boat, or any other means of transportation. Wherever they walk, I pray that their feet do not slip; lead them far away from danger (Psalm 17:5). Keep them safe at all times. I pray that You will be their "refuge and strength" and their "very present help in trouble" (Psalm 46:1). I pray that no weapon formed against them will prosper (Isaiah 54:17).

In Jesus' name I pray.

Though I walk through the valley of the shadow of death, I will fear no evil; for You are with me; Your rod and Your staff, they comfort me.

Psalm 23:4

Prayer Notes

Pray That Your Adult Children Will

Be Protected and Survive Tough Times

Lord, You have said in Your Word that even though evil people try to destroy the righteous, You will not allow it (Psalm 37:32-33). Protect my adult children from any plans of evil. Protect them from legal problems, for justice comes from You (Proverbs 29:26). Be with them when they pass through deep waters and keep the river from overflowing them. Enable them to not be burned or consumed in the fire (Isaiah 43:2). Be merciful to them and give them safety "in the shadow of Your wings" until such time as all "these calamities have passed by" (Psalm 57:1). Give them the wisdom, discernment, and revelation they need in order to stay safe.

In Jesus' name I pray.

*When you pass through the waters, I will be
with you; and through the rivers, they shall not
overflow you. When you walk through the fire, you
shall not be burned, nor shall the flame scorch you.*

ISAIAH 43:2

Prayer Notes

Pray That Your Adult Children Will

Be Protected and Survive Tough Times

Lord, I pray when my adult children go through tough times that You will be their defender. I pray that they will learn to look to You to be their help (Psalm 121:1-2). The enemy's strength is nothing in light of Your great power. I pray that they will learn to cry out to You in their trouble, so You will deliver them out of their distresses (Psalm 107:6). No matter what happens, I pray they will ultimately be able to say, "This was the LORD's doing; it is marvelous in our eyes" (Psalm 118:23). Help them to understand that they can "lie down in peace, and sleep; for You alone, O LORD," make them to "dwell in safety" (Psalm 4:8).

In Jesus' name I pray.

The LORD is my rock and my fortress
and my deliverer; my God, my strength,
in whom I will trust; my shield and the horn
of my salvation, my stronghold.

PSALM 18:2

Prayer Notes

Pray That Your Adult Children Will

Recognize Their
Need for God

Lord, I pray for (<u>name of adult child</u>) that You would help her (him) recognize her (his) need for You. Help her (him) to understand that You know her (his) needs even better than she (he) does (Luke 12:29-30). Teach her (him) to seek You as her (his) hiding place and hope (Psalm 119:114). Strengthen her (him) to choose to keep Your commandments and "depart" from those who would lead her (him) away from You (Psalm 119:115). I pray You would teach her (him) Your ways— "as Your custom is toward those who love Your name" (Psalm 119:124,132). Help me to live Your way and to model clearly what utter dependence on You looks like, so she (he) will be inspired to walk in that same way (1 John 5:2).

In Jesus' name I pray.

As the deer pants for the water brooks,
so pants my soul for You, O God.
My soul thirsts for God, for the living God.

PSALM 42:1-2

Prayer Notes

_____

_____

_____

_____

_____

_____

_____

_____

_____

_____

_____

Pray That Your Adult Children Will

Walk into the Future God Has for Them

Lord, I pray for (<u>name of adult child</u>) to have a future that is good, long, prosperous, and secure because it is in Your hands. Thank You that Your thoughts toward him (her) are thoughts of peace and to give him (her) a future and a hope (Jeremiah 29:11). Turn his (her) heart toward You so that he (she) always has Your will and Your ways in mind. Keep him (her) from wasting time on a pathway that You will not bless. Help him (her) to run the race in the right way, so that he (she) will finish strong and receive the prize You have for him (her) (1 Corinthians 9:24). I pray that nothing will ever separate him (her) from You (Romans 8:38-39).

In Jesus' name I pray.

Mark the blameless man,
and observe the upright;
for the future of that man is peace.

PSALM 37:37

Prayer Notes

Pray That Your Adult Children Will

Walk into the Future God Has for Them

Lord, I pray that my adult child will be planted firmly in Your house so that he (she) will always be fresh and flourishing and bear fruit into old age (Psalm 92:13-15). Help him (her) to remember that You are "able to do exceedingly abundantly above all that we ask or think, according to the power that works in us" (Ephesians 3:20). Guide him (her) step-by-step so that he (she) never gets off the path You have for his (her) life. I pray that You—the God of hope—will fill him (her) with Your joy and peace so that he (she) will "abound in hope by the power of the Holy Spirit" (Romans 15:13).

In Jesus' name I pray.

Eye has not seen, nor ear heard, nor have entered into the heart of man the things which God has prepared for those who love Him.

1 Corinthians 2:9

Prayer Notes

Other Books by Stormie Omartian

THE POWER OF A PRAYING® PARENT

Learn how to turn to the Lord and place every detail of your child's life in *His* hands by praying for such things as your child's safety, character development, peer pressure, friends, family relationships, and much more. Discover the joy of being part of God's work in your child's life. You don't have to be a perfect parent. You just need to be a praying parent.

PRAYER WARRIOR

Stormie says, "There is already a war going on around you, and you are in it whether you want to be or not. There is a spiritual war of good and evil—between God and His enemy—and God wants us to stand strong on His side, the side that wins. We win the war when we pray in power because prayer *is* the battle." This book will help you become a powerful prayer warrior who understands the path to victory.

LEAD ME, HOLY SPIRIT

Stormie has written books on prayer that have helped millions of people talk to God. Now she focuses on the Holy Spirit and how He wants you to listen to His gentle leading when He speaks to your heart, soul, and spirit. He wants to help you enter into the relationship with God you yearn for and the wholeness and freedom He has for you. He wants to lead you into a better life than you could ever possibly live without Him.